GROWING WITH CHRIST

30 DAY YOUTH PRAYER JOURNAL

AMANDA BALL-KNIGHT

Scripture quotations taken from the King James Version of the Bible.

WestBow Press books may be ordered through booksellers or by contacting:

WestBow Press
A Division of Thomas Nelson & Zondervan
1663 Liberty Drive
Bloomington, IN 47403
www.westbowpress.com
1 (866) 928-1240

ISBN: 978-1-9736-6141-2 (sc)

Library of Congress Control Number: 2019905919

Print information available on the last page.

WestBow Press rev. date: 06/03/2019

WESTBOW
P R E S S®
A DIVISION OF THOMAS NELSON
& ZONDERVAN

This book is dedicated to three very special Sunday School teachers who helped guide me in my Christian walk,

Debbie Minton,
Darrell Lear, &
Tom Cornette.

Also, for my children, Maggye and Halbert, may you always draw near to the Lord!

Hello dear friend!! Yes, you reading this! I am so excited that you chose to grow your relationship with Christ through prayer.

It is so important that we each take time out of every day to spend quality time alone with God. God desires that we communicate with Him. God created us to communicate with Him and to worship Him. Prayer is communication with God. It shouldn't just be reciting a memorized prayer or it shouldn't be a list of wants and demands, but prayer is just talking with God. God desires that of us, just as we talk and communicate with our friends and family.

Jesus shows us the importance of spending one on one time with God in the scripture...

Matthew 14:23
"And when he had sent the multitudes away, he went up into a mountain apart to pray: and when the evening was come, he was there alone."

This scripture tells us that even Jesus went apart (by Himself) to pray. Spending alone time with God is the key to spiritual power and growth. Having a personal relationship with Christ is vital to our spiritual growth. We should spend time talking with Christ every day, as well as opening our heart to listen to what Christ is saying to us.

This 30 Day Youth Prayer Journal offers you space to express yourself. Write out your thoughts, prayer requests, and praises. There are writing prompts for each day to inspire your writing, a doodle page so get creative, and a page to journal out your daily prayer. There is also a daily Bible verse to help you learn God's Holy Word and a place to journal your thoughts on the verse. Three pages are included for each day.

The pages of this journal are black and white, so you have complete creative control. Get out your crayons, colored pencils, gel pens, or whatever you like to use to create! Have fun and let God inspire you as you pray and use your creative ability!!

I have faithfully prayed over this journal that it will touch your heart and help you grow closer to Christ through prayer.

Dear Heavenly Father,
I ask you to touch the one reading this journal. That you will lead them on an incredible journey with you, as they grow spiritually and strengthen their prayer life. I ask you to open their heart and mind to be reverent, obedient, and receptive to your sweet Holy Spirit. In Jesus' Name, Amen.

The most important prayer you can pray is to ask Jesus into your heart and to accept Him as your personal Saviour!!   Doing this is as easy as ABC!

A- *Admit you are a sinner in need of a Saviour*

B- *Believe that Jesus died on the cross and rose again on the third day*

C- *Confess that Jesus is your Saviour and Continue to follow Him*

Here are some scriptures that are commonly referred to as the Roman Road. Read and study these scriptures, and they will help guide you in your salvation journey.

Road To Salvation

Romans 3:10
No one is perfect.

Romans 3:23
All have sinned.

Romans 6:23
Sin is death, but Jesus is life.

Romans 5:8
Christ died for our sins.

Romans 10:9-10
Confess & believe to be saved.

Romans 10:13
Call on the Lord to be saved.

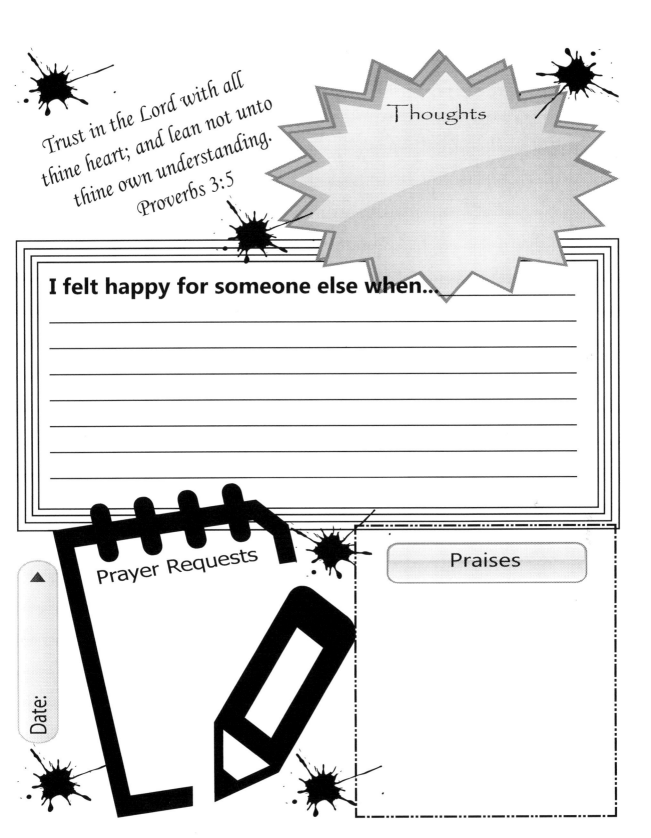

Trust in the Lord with all thine heart; and lean not unto thine own understanding.
Proverbs 3:5

Thoughts

I felt happy for someone else when...

Prayer Requests

Praises

Date:

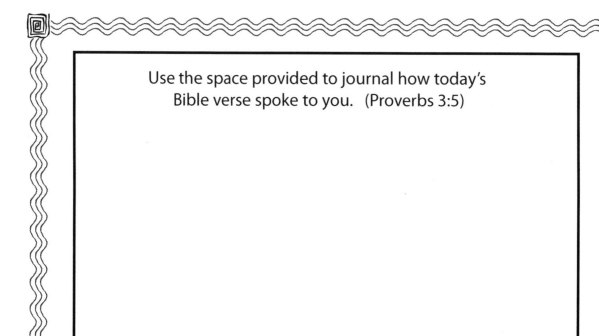

Use the space provided to journal how today's
Bible verse spoke to you.   (Proverbs 3:5)

Doodles

Dear Heavenly Father,

_____

_____

_____

_____

_____

_____

_____

_____

_____

_____

_____

_____

_____

_____

_____

_____

_____

_____In Jesus' Name, Amen

Jesus Christ the same yesterday, and to day, and for ever.
Hebrews 13:8

Thoughts

I felt good about myself when...

Prayer Requests

Praises

Date:

Use the space provided to journal how today's
Bible verse spoke to you.   (Hebrews 13:8)

Doodles

Dear Heavenly Father,

_____

_____

_____

_____

_____

_____

_____

_____

_____

_____

_____

_____

_____

_____

_____

_____

_____

_____

_____

_____In Jesus' Name, Amen

Let every thing that hath breath praise the Lord. Praise ye the Lord. Psalms 150:6

Thoughts

Something I did for someone...

Prayer Requests

Praises

Date:

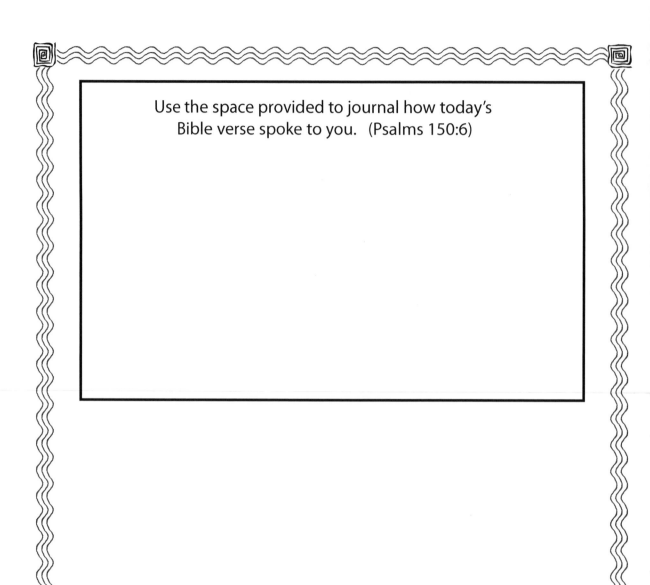

Use the space provided to journal how today's
Bible verse spoke to you.   (Psalms 150:6)

Doodles

Dear Heavenly Father,

_____

_____

_____

_____

_____

_____

_____

_____

_____

_____

_____

_____

_____

_____

_____

_____

_____

_____

_____In Jesus' Name, Amen

Set your affection on things above, not on things on the earth. Colossians 3:2

Thoughts

I had fun when...

Prayer Requests

Date:

Praises

Use the space provided to journal how today's
Bible verse spoke to you.   (Colossians 3:2)

Doodles

Dear Heavenly Father,

_____

_____

_____

_____

_____

_____

_____

_____

_____

_____

_____

_____

_____

_____

_____

_____

_____

_____

_____In Jesus' Name, Amen

The Lord bless thee, and keep thee:
Numbers 6:24

Thoughts

Describe an event that changed your life forever...

Prayer Requests

Praises

Date:

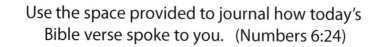

Use the space provided to journal how today's
Bible verse spoke to you.   (Numbers 6:24)

Doodles

Dear Heavenly Father,

_____

_____

_____

_____

_____

_____

_____

_____

_____

_____

_____

_____

_____

_____

_____

_____

_____

_____

_____In Jesus' Name, Amen

I can do all things through
Christ which strengtheneth me.
Philippians 4:13

Thoughts

I felt happy when...

Prayer Requests

Praises

Date:

Use the space provided to journal how today's
Bible verse spoke to you.   (Philippians 4:13)

Doodles

Dear Heavenly Father,

_____
_____
_____
_____
_____
_____
_____
_____
_____
_____
_____
_____
_____
_____
_____
_____
_____
_____
_____
_____In Jesus' Name, Amen

Thy word is a lamp unto my feet, and a light unto my path.
Psalms 119:105

Thoughts

Free writing...

Prayer Requests

Praises

Date:

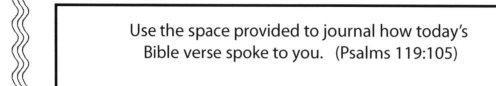

Use the space provided to journal how today's
Bible verse spoke to you.   (Psalms 119:105)

Doodles

Dear Heavenly Father,

_____

_____

_____

_____

_____

_____

_____

_____

_____

_____

_____

_____

_____

_____

_____

_____

_____

_____

_____In Jesus' Name, Amen

And they said, Believe on the Lord Jesus Christ, and thou shalt be saved, and thy house.
Acts 16:31

Thoughts

What is something kind you can do for someone else... _____

_____

_____

_____

_____

_____

_____

Prayer Requests

Praises

Date:

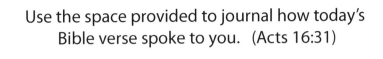

Use the space provided to journal how today's
Bible verse spoke to you. (Acts 16:31)

Doodles

Dear Heavenly Father,

_____
_____
_____
_____
_____
_____
_____
_____
_____
_____
_____
_____
_____
_____
_____
_____
_____
_____
_____
_____In Jesus' Name, Amen

This is the day which the Lord hath made; we will rejoice and be glad in it.
Psalms 118:24

Thoughts

Something I did well today... _____

_____
_____
_____
_____
_____
_____

Prayer Requests

Praises

Date:

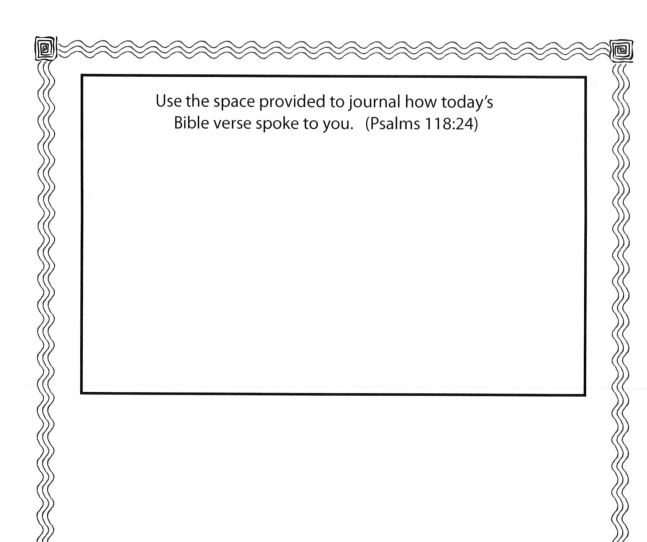

Use the space provided to journal how today's
Bible verse spoke to you.   (Psalms 118:24)

Doodles

Dear Heavenly Father,

_____

_____

_____

_____

_____

_____

_____

_____

_____

_____

_____

_____

_____

_____

_____

_____

_____

_____In Jesus' Name, Amen

And as ye would that men should do to you, do ye should do to them likewise.
Luke 6:31

Thoughts

Something positive about today...

Prayer Requests

Praises

Date:

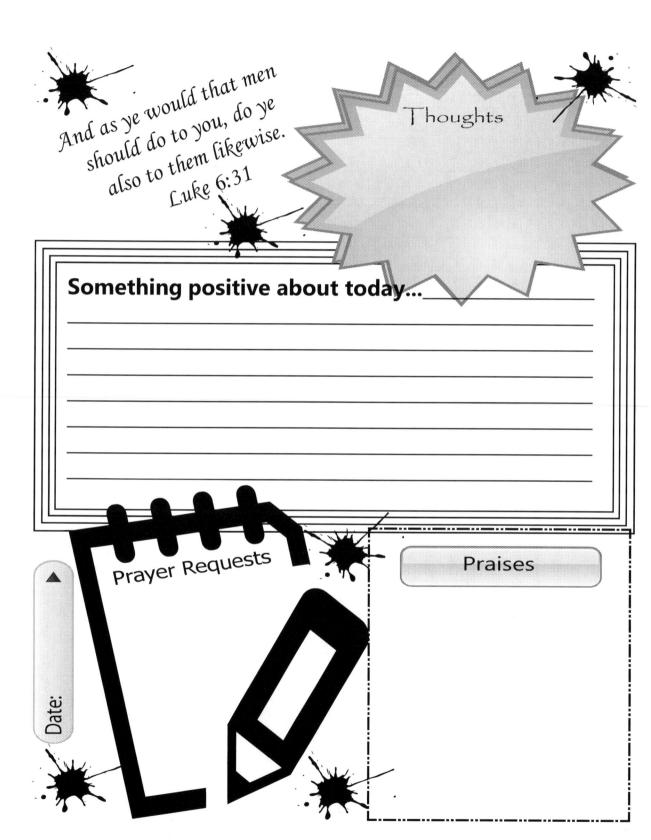

Use the space provided to journal how today's
Bible verse spoke to you.   (Luke 6:31)

Doodles

Dear Heavenly Father,

_____

_____

_____

_____

_____

_____

_____

_____

_____

_____

_____

_____

_____

_____

_____

_____

_____

_____

_____In Jesus' Name, Amen

In the beginning God created the heaven and the earth.
Genesis 1:1

Thoughts

Today was interesting because...

Prayer Requests

Praises

Date:

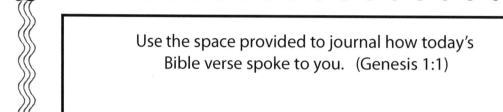

Use the space provided to journal how today's
Bible verse spoke to you.   (Genesis 1:1)

Doodles

Dear Heavenly Father,

_____

_____

_____

_____

_____

_____

_____

_____

_____

_____

_____

_____

_____

_____

_____

_____

_____

_____

_____

_____

_____In Jesus' Name, Amen

Finally, my brethren, be strong in the Lord, and in the power of his might.
Ephesians 6:10

Thoughts

Describe someone who is a hero to you and explain why... _____
_____
_____
_____
_____
_____
_____

Prayer Requests

Praises

Date:

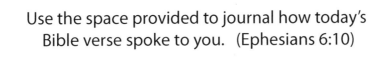

Use the space provided to journal how today's
Bible verse spoke to you.   (Ephesians 6:10)

Doodles

Dear Heavenly Father,

_____

_____

_____

_____

_____

_____

_____

_____

_____

_____

_____

_____

_____

_____

_____

_____

_____

_____

_____

_____In Jesus' Name, Amen

Pray without ceasing.
1 Thessalonians 5:17

Thoughts

Three goals I have set for myself are...

Prayer Requests

Date:

Praises

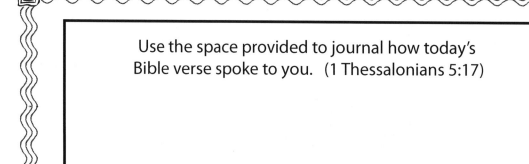

Use the space provided to journal how today's Bible verse spoke to you.   (1 Thessalonians 5:17)

Doodles

Dear Heavenly Father,

_____

_____

_____

_____

_____

_____

_____

_____

_____

_____

_____

_____

_____

_____

_____

_____

_____

_____

_____In Jesus' Name, Amen

Trust ye in the Lord for ever:
for in the Lord Jehovah
is everlasting strength:
Isaiah 26:4

Thoughts

Free writing... _____

Prayer Requests

Praises

Date:

Use the space provided to journal how today's
Bible verse spoke to you.   (Isaiah 26:4)

Doodles

Dear Heavenly Father,

_____

_____

_____

_____

_____

_____

_____

_____

_____

_____

_____

_____

_____

_____

_____

_____

_____

_____

_____In Jesus' Name, Amen

Wherefore, my beloved brethren, let every man be swift to hear, slow to speak, slow to wrath:
James 1:19

Thoughts

Write about a smell that sparks a memory...

Prayer Requests

Praises

Date:

47

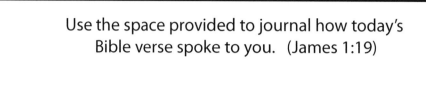

Use the space provided to journal how today's
Bible verse spoke to you.   (James 1:19)

Doodles

Dear Heavenly Father,

_____

_____

_____

_____

_____

_____

_____

_____

_____

_____

_____

_____

_____

_____

_____

_____

_____

_____

_____ In Jesus' Name, Amen

What time I am afraid,
I will trust in thee.
Psalms 56:3

Thoughts

Write about a time in your life when you struggled with a choice and what you did..._____

_____
_____
_____
_____
_____
_____

Prayer Requests

Praises

Date:

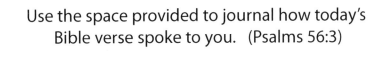

Use the space provided to journal how today's
Bible verse spoke to you.   (Psalms 56:3)

Doodles

Dear Heavenly Father,

_____

_____

_____

_____

_____

_____

_____

_____

_____

_____

_____

_____

_____

_____

_____

_____

_____

_____

_____In Jesus' Name, Amen

Now the Lord is that Spirit: and where the Spirit of the Lord is, there is liberty.
2 Corinthians 3:17

Thoughts

What does the word family mean to you...

_____
_____
_____
_____
_____
_____
_____
_____

Prayer Requests

Praises

Date:

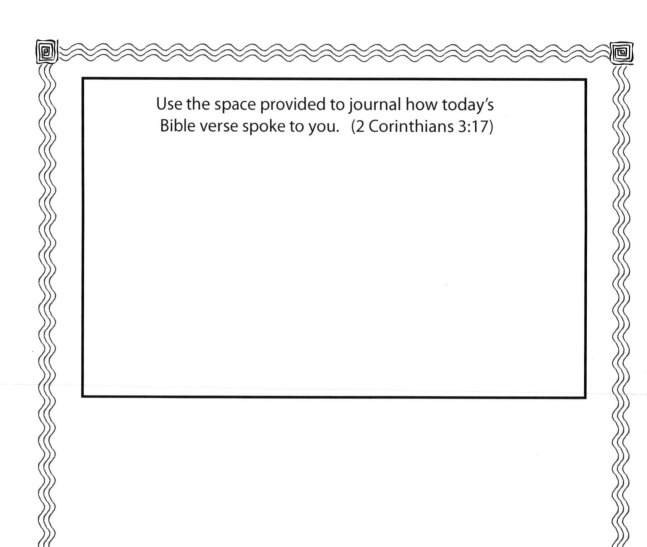

Use the space provided to journal how today's
Bible verse spoke to you.   (2 Corinthians 3:17)

Doodles

Dear Heavenly Father,

_____

_____

_____

_____

_____

_____

_____

_____

_____

_____

_____

_____

_____

_____

_____

_____

_____

_____In Jesus' Name, Amen

Be strong and of a good courage, fear not, nor be afraid of them: for the Lord thy God, he it is that doth go with thee; he will not fail thee, nor forsake thee.
Deuteronomy 31:6

Thoughts

My greatest memory...

Prayer Requests

Praises

Date:

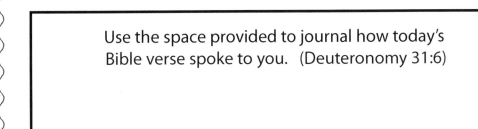

Use the space provided to journal how today's
Bible verse spoke to you. (Deuteronomy 31:6)

Doodles

Dear Heavenly Father,

_____

_____

_____

_____

_____

_____

_____

_____

_____

_____

_____

_____

_____

_____

_____

_____

_____

_____

_____In Jesus' Name, Amen

For God so loved the world, that he gave his only begotten Son, that whosoever believeth in him should not perish, but have everlasting life.
John 3:16

Thoughts

My best day was...

_____

_____

_____

_____

_____

_____

_____

Prayer Requests

Praises

Date:

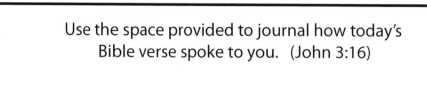

Use the space provided to journal how today's
Bible verse spoke to you.   (John 3:16)

Doodles

Dear Heavenly Father,

_____

_____

_____

_____

_____

_____

_____

_____

_____

_____

_____

_____

_____

_____

_____

_____

_____

_____

_____In Jesus' Name, Amen

And whatsoever ye do in word or deed,
do all in the name of the Lord Jesus,
giving thanks to God and the Father by him.
Colossians 3:17

Thoughts

What are three symbols or objects that represent you...

Prayer Requests

Praises

Date:

62

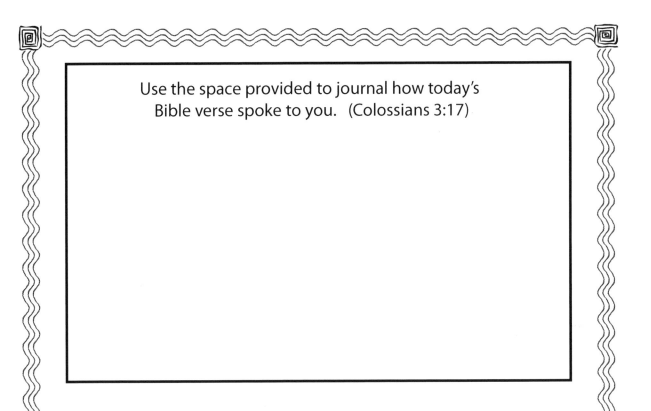

Use the space provided to journal how today's
Bible verse spoke to you.   (Colossians 3:17)

Doodles

Dear Heavenly Father,

_____

_____

_____

_____

_____

_____

_____

_____

_____

_____

_____

_____

_____

_____

_____

_____

_____

_____

_____In Jesus' Name, Amen

For I the Lord thy God will hold thy right hand, saying unto thee, Fear not; I will help thee.
Isaiah 41:13

Thoughts

Free writing... _____
_____
_____
_____
_____
_____
_____
_____
_____

Prayer Requests

Praises

Date:

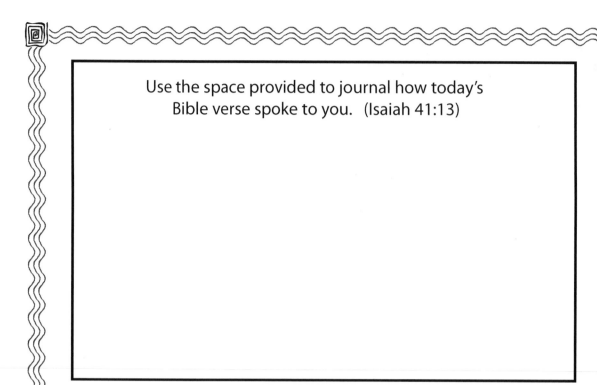

Use the space provided to journal how today's
Bible verse spoke to you. (Isaiah 41:13)

Doodles

Dear Heavenly Father,

_____

_____

_____

_____

_____

_____

_____

_____

_____

_____

_____

_____

_____

_____

_____

_____

_____

_____

_____In Jesus' Name, Amen

For we are his workmanship, created in Christ Jesus unto good works, which God hath before ordained that we should walk in them.

Ephesians 2:10

Thoughts

Write about a disappointment...

Prayer Requests

Praises

Date:

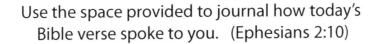
Use the space provided to journal how today's
Bible verse spoke to you.   (Ephesians 2:10)

Doodles

Dear Heavenly Father,

_____

_____

_____

_____

_____

_____

_____

_____

_____

_____

_____

_____

_____

_____

_____

_____

_____

_____In Jesus' Name, Amen

O give thanks unto the Lord; for he is good: for his mercy endureth for ever.
Psalms 136:1

Thoughts

Five years from now, I will be...

Date:

Prayer Requests

Praises

71

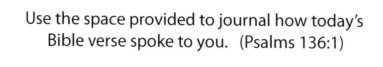

Use the space provided to journal how today's
Bible verse spoke to you.   (Psalms 136:1)

Doodles

Dear Heavenly Father,

_____

_____

_____

_____

_____

_____

_____

_____

_____

_____

_____

_____

_____

_____

_____

_____

_____

_____In Jesus' Name, Amen

*Rejoice in the Lord always:
and again I say, Rejoice.
Philippians 4:4*

Thoughts

Today I accomplished...

Prayer Requests

Praises

Date:

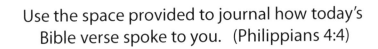

Use the space provided to journal how today's
Bible verse spoke to you.   (Philippians 4:4)

Doodles

Dear Heavenly Father,

_____

_____

_____

_____

_____

_____

_____

_____

_____

_____

_____

_____

_____

_____

_____

_____

_____

_____

_____In Jesus' Name, Amen

Wherefore thou art great, O Lord God: for there is none like thee, neither is there any God beside thee, according to all that we have heard with our ears.

2 Samuel 7:22

Thoughts

I was inspired by... _____

_____
_____
_____
_____
_____
_____
_____
_____
_____

Prayer Requests

Praises

Date:

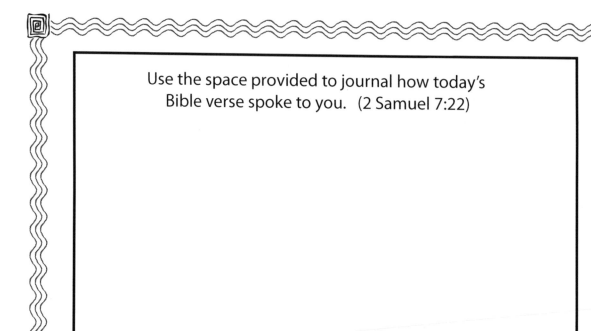

Use the space provided to journal how today's
Bible verse spoke to you.   (2 Samuel 7:22)

Doodles

Dear Heavenly Father,

_____

_____

_____

_____

_____

_____

_____

_____

_____

_____

_____

_____

_____

_____

_____

_____

_____

_____In Jesus' Name, Amen

That if thou shalt confess with thy mouth the Lord Jesus, and shalt believe in thine heart that God hath raised him from the dead, thou shalt be saved.

Romans 10:9

Thoughts

Were you ever accused of something that you didn't do? How did you feel...

_____

_____

_____

_____

_____

_____

_____

Prayer Requests

Praises

Date:

Use the space provided to journal how today's
Bible verse spoke to you.   (Romans 10:9)

Doodles

Dear Heavenly Father,

_____

_____

_____

_____

_____

_____

_____

_____

_____

_____

_____

_____

_____

_____

_____

_____

_____

_____

_____In Jesus' Name, Amen

Blessed be the Lord, who daily loadeth us with benefits, even the God of our salvation. Selah.
Psalms 68:19

Thoughts

What does the word promise mean to you...

Prayer Requests

Praises

Date:

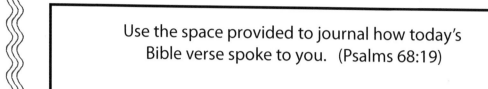

Use the space provided to journal how today's
Bible verse spoke to you.   (Psalms 68:19)

Doodles

Dear Heavenly Father,

_____

_____

_____

_____

_____

_____

_____

_____

_____

_____

_____

_____

_____

_____

_____

_____

_____

_____In Jesus' Name, Amen

Submit yourselves therefore to God. Resist the devil, and he will flee from you.
James 4:7

Thoughts

Free writing... _____

_____
_____
_____
_____
_____
_____
_____
_____

Prayer Requests

Praises

Date:

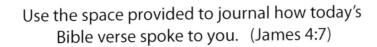

Use the space provided to journal how today's
Bible verse spoke to you. (James 4:7)

Doodles

Dear Heavenly Father,

_____

_____

_____

_____

_____

_____

_____

_____

_____

_____

_____

_____

_____

_____

_____

_____

_____

_____

_____

_____In Jesus' Name, Amen

Looking unto Jesus the author and finisher of our faith; who for the joy that was set before him endured the cross, despising the shame, and is set down at the right hand of the throne of God.
Hebrews 12:2

Thoughts

Write a poem about prayer...

_____
_____
_____
_____
_____
_____
_____

Prayer Requests

Date:

Praises

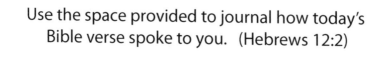

Use the space provided to journal how today's
Bible verse spoke to you. (Hebrews 12:2)

Doodles

Dear Heavenly Father,

_____

_____

_____

_____

_____

_____

_____

_____

_____

_____

_____

_____

_____

_____

_____

_____

_____

_____In Jesus' Name, Amen

The Lord is good to all:
and his tender mercies are
over all his works.
Psalms 145:9

Thoughts

Write your favorite Bible verse...

Prayer Requests

Praises

Date:

Use the space provided to journal how today's
Bible verse spoke to you.   (Psalms 145:9)

Doodles

Dear Heavenly Father,

_____

_____

_____

_____

_____

_____

_____

_____

_____

_____

_____

_____

_____

_____

_____

_____

_____

_____In Jesus' Name, Amen

Share in the space provided how your prayer life has grown after reading and journaling through this "Growing With Christ" 30 Day Youth Prayer Journal.

_____

_____

_____

_____

_____

_____

_____

_____

_____

_____

_____

I hope this "Growing With Christ" 30 Day Youth Prayer Journal has been a blessing to you!! On the next page, you will find a 30 Day Prayer Challenge. Each day includes a topic, a scripture to read, and a prayer prompt to begin your prayer. I encourage you to take the next 30 days and continue to grow your relationship with Christ through prayer.

Then shall ye call upon me, and ye shall go and pray unto me, and I will hearken unto you.
Jeremiah 29:12

Rejoicing in hope; patient in tribulation; continuing instant in prayer;
Romans 12:12

Gratitude
(Ephesians 5:20)

Lord help me live a life where I am thankful in all things in the name of Jesus.

Contentment
(Philippians 4:12-13)

Lord teach me to be content in all situations through the strength given by Christ.

Godly Friends
(Ecclesiastes 4:9-12)

Lord guide me in friendships where we encourage one another and help one another grow in Spirit.

Love
(Ephesians 5:2)

Lord guide me to love others the way you love me.

Unity
(Ephesians 4:3)

Lord help me keep my mind on you and be in unity with the Holy Spirit.

Mercy
(Luke 6:36)

May I always show mercy just as Christ has shown me mercy.

Faith
(Matthew 17:20)

Lord continue to increase my faith that it may grow in my heart, so I will know with you nothing is impossible.

Respect
(1 Peter 2:17)

Lord guide me in showing respect to everyone, just as your Word commands.

Generosity
(1 Timothy 6:18)

Lord mold in my heart a willingness to share and to give to others.

Kindness
(Ephesians 4:32)

Lord guide me to always be kind to everyone.

Health
(1 Corinthians 6:19)

Lord always guide me to use my body to glorify you and that you will bless my health.

Wisdom
(Proverbs 4:7)

Lord increase my wisdom in you.

Desire to Pray
(Ephesians 6:18 / Matthew 6:9-13)

Lord teach me to pray and have a desire to pray in all things.

Honesty
(Psalms 25:21)

May honesty be my virtue.

Courage
(Deuteronomy 31:6)

Lord strengthen my faith that I will always be courageous knowing that you are continuously by my side.

Godly Words
(Ephesians 4:29)

Lord guide my thoughts and speech, that whatever I say will build up and encourage.

Peace
(Colossians 3:15)

Lord let me chase after Godly peace and may it lead my heart.

Strength
(Isaiah 40:29)

Lord remind me that I draw my strength from you.

Purity
(Psalms 51:10)

Lord create in me a pure heart that I may be pure in all things.

Joy
(1 Thessalonians 1:6)

Lord fill me with the joy from the Holy Spirit.

Fruit of the Spirit
(Galatians 5:22-23)

Lord help me grow so that I may be fruitful with things of you.

Humble
(James 4:6)

Lord help me not to have a prideful heart, that I may always remain humble.

Salvation
(Romans 10:9-13)

Dear Lord, please forgive me and come into my heart as my personal Saviour. Help me walk closely in your footsteps. I love you.

Work for Christ
(Colossians 3:23)

Lord teach me to work hard and always work like I am working for you.

Rooted
(Colossians 2:7)

Lord help me keep my faith rooted in you.

Protection
(2 Thessalonians 3:3)

Lord help my heart to always know that you are my protector.

Commitment
(Psalms 37:5)

Lord I commit my life to you. Guide me in your ways.

Self-esteem
(Ephesians 2:10)

Lord guide me in growing my self-esteem, that I will always know my worth is rooted in you because I am a masterpiece created by you.

Purpose
(Jeremiah 1:5)

Lord always let me remember that I was created on purpose, with purpose, and for a purpose.

Servants Heart
(Ephesians 6:7)

Lord mold in me a servants heart, that I will serve wholeheartedly for you.

Special Acknowledgements

Maggye Knight created the cover of this "Growing With Christ" 30 Day Youth Prayer Journal. Maggye is the daughter of author Amanda Ball-Knight and Rev. Joe Knight. She enjoys spending her free time creating works of art and cheerleading. This is the second book in which Maggye's artwork has been featured.

Maggye created this art piece in the 2018 "The Hungry Artist" Summer Art Camp. The Hungry Artist was founded by artist Mary Ann French and is based on the scripture Matthew 5:6.

Pictured below is Maggye Knight and Mary Ann French holding Maggye's treasured artwork.

Printed in the United States
By Bookmasters